I0657263

Gallery Books
Editor: Peter Fallon

EXIT / ENTRANCE

Aidan Mathews

EXIT/ENTRANCE

Gallery Books

Exit / Entrance
is first published
simultaneously in paperback
and in a clothbound edition
in November 1990.

The Gallery Press
Loughcrew
Oldcastle
County Meath
Ireland

© Aidan Mathews 1988, 1990

ISBN 1 85235 054 7 (*paperback*)
1 85235 055 5 (*clothbound*)

The publisher acknowledges gratefully the efforts of Ben Barnes to see this play in print.

All rights whatsoever in this play are strictly reserved and applications for performance etc. should be made before rehearsal to A. P. Watt, 20 John Street, London WC1N 2DR.

The Gallery Press receives financial assistance from An Chomhairle Ealaíon / The Arts Council, Ireland

for Arthur Lappin

Exit/Entrance was first produced by Arthur Lappin in association with the Abbey Theatre in the Peacock Theatre, Dublin, on 2 February 1988, with the following cast:

Exit

CHARLES, *an invalid, perhaps 70*   Denys Hawthorne
HELEN, *his wife, probably 65*   Joan O'Hara

Entrance

CHARLES, *a young man, perhaps 30*   Malcolm Douglas
HELEN, *his lover, probably 25*   Ingrid Craigie

Director: Ben Barnes
Set and costume design: Tim Reed
Lighting design: Rupert Murray

The action takes place in the living-room of an apartment in a period town-house.

EXIT

Scene 1: Six O'Clock

The living room of an apartment in a period town-house. A suite of furniture at centre-stage. Two wall-lights, one on each side of the fireplace mantel to the right. Two standard lamps, one behind the couch, the other at left beside a ceiling-to-floor bookcase which extends along the left wall and the back wall to a panelled door. Table at left foreground, on which neat heaps of paper are piled.

HELEN *is sitting on the couch, upright, hands in lap, staring into fireplace. Car headlights from outside travel as if through Venetian blinds across the room from left to right. The 'phone, on a small table at the door, begins to ring.* HELEN *can't decide what to do, walks across the room back and forth. Car headlights stop. 'Phone goes on ringing. Helen sits down again, draws a cardigan round her shoulders, sways her torso like a child in pain towards her lap, up again. Sounds at door.* CHARLES *enters, stands in doorway looking at her. 'Phone still ringing. They look at each other.*

CHARLES No.

> *Pause.*

HELEN Perhaps —
CHARLES No.
HELEN If it's Philip —
CHARLES Why would it be Philip?
HELEN It could be.
CHARLES When has Philip rung?
HELEN Only Philip would ring that long.

> *'Phone stops abruptly. Silence.* CHARLES *closes the door behind him.*

9

CHARLES   I have everything. What we need.

HELEN   I know. I know you do. (*Pause*) He rang two weeks
ago.

CHARLES   Tight. He was tight. I could hear people laughing. And
somebody shushing them.

HELEN   He meant well.

CHARLES   (*Walks to table, stands looking down at papers, shifts one
or two*) Hap-py anni-versary.

HELEN   He was only a day out.

CHARLES   Two. Not that it matters.

HELEN   You take things so personally. You take things so
much to heart.

CHARLES   Insults are nothing. But a trivial insult . . . (*Pause*) It
will be all right. I do promise.

HELEN   I know.

'Phone rings. HELEN *turns to look at* CHARLES.

HELEN   That —

CHARLES   Somebody else.

HELEN   But perhaps —

CHARLES   The wrong number.

HELEN   I suppose so.

CHARLES   One in a million.

HELEN   We should have taken it off the hook. We should have
anticipated this . . . .

CHARLES   Contingency. Con-tingo, con-tingere.

HELEN   Who else rings us?

CHARLES   The friend of a friend who left here months ago. From
above, from below, from down the corridor. Rent
owing.

HELEN   Please answer it.

CHARLES   Or one of my students, in search of some crucial
footnote from a German dissertation on the com-
pound epithet in Hesiod.

HELEN   For me.

CHARLES   (*More loudly*) Or a salesman offering reduced rates on
a sensor alarm system.

HELEN   For yourself then.

CHARLES   Or whatever.

HELEN Or Philip.

'Phone stops ringing. Silence.

CHARLES You see the humour. An alarm system — to shut out trespassers, misfits, pickpockets, burglars, rapists, squatters. (*Pause*) Grave-robbers.
HELEN Or your only son.

Pause. Then sudden, staccato hammering from behind bookcase on left wall.

CHARLES Now what?
HELEN It's the new couple. I met them yesterday. Young, pink from the cold, frozen hands. And excited.

Hammering stops.

CHARLES A laugh a minute.
HELEN Carting in pots and pans, and skillets, and a big wooden clothes horse. Two tea-chests in the hall, jam-packed. Speakers, and little things wrapped in newspaper. And the smell of tea in the hall, from the tea-chests. It smelled like Java. (*Emphatically*) 'How are you?' they asked me. (*Exaggeratedly*) 'How are you?'
CHARLES And you?
HELEN Oh, I said . . . (*Pause*) 'Don't be scared of all the speakers,' he said, the young man. About Philip's age, a little older, very bad skin, but a nice face. 'We're a very retiring couple,' he said.
CHARLES And you?
HELEN Oh, I said . . . (*Pause*) 'Our orgies are always discreet,' he said; and she punched him with the end of her scarf wrapped round her hand, punched his shoulder, and they giggled.
CHARLES This is terribly . . . affecting.
HELEN (*Simply*) I thought it was —
CHARLES (*Tenderly*) Rather nice, to be honest.
HELEN Rather nice, to be honest.

Silence. Car headlights cross the room from right to left.

You know.
CHARLES Hmm?
HELEN I wished them well.
CHARLES That was daring.
HELEN (*Surprised at herself*) But I meant it.

They look at each other.

Scene 2: Seven O'Clock

As before. HELEN *is sitting on the couch,* CHARLES *on the single chair at right angles to it. They have been drinking.*

HELEN   I feel . . . . strange.

CHARLES   Don't be tiddly. Don't be.

HELEN   I'm not tiddly.

CHARLES   There must be . . . there must be (*floundering*) a sense of . . . dignity, I suppose.

HELEN   But I don't know . . .

CHARLES   We should talk about . . . happenings, things that have happened. (*More decisively*) We should talk about people, places, faces, details, ourselves. Whatnot. Whatever.

HELEN   Whatever.

CHARLES   Holidays. Moments. Events that mattered. Experiences. There's so much. (*Pause*) But it has to be done properly.

HELEN   Do you want me to start?

CHARLES   Not like that. It has to be spontaneous. It has to come of itself. You can't just . . . arrange it.

Car headlights cross the room from left to right.

HELEN   Our honeymoon.

CHARLES   Why there?

HELEN   Didn't it start there? Wasn't that a start? You have to start somewhere.

CHARLES   Of course. Of course you have to start somewhere. But you can start anywhere. You can start . . . today. This moment. Here. Now. You can start in the uterus. You can start at the first day. You can start with alpha. Everything is a beginning. (*Pause*) In a way. (*Pause*) In its own way.

HELEN   Our honeymoon.

CHARLES   All right. Our honeymoon. My birth. Your birth. Philip's birth. My first book. My last book. (*Pause*) The operation. (*Pause*) Any of them.

HELEN   The breakdown. My breakdown.

CHARLES   It wasn't a breakdown.

HELEN   My tiredness.

CHARLES   It was a tiredness.

HELEN   But a quietness too. Never so quiet. The starched aprons of nurses like . . . newspaper being crushed. Their shoes in the corridor: great wallops. Wallop, flop. Wallop, flop.

CHARLES   A tiredness.

HELEN   The sounds of your body. Mutterings. All day long, your stomach juices, your heartbeat. All night long. And whiteness. Everything so white.

CHARLES   A great fatigue.

HELEN   White is my favourite. Our honeymoon was white. (*Pause*) Everything about it.

CHARLES   Your dress.

HELEN   Not that. Not the wedding. The honeymoon. (*Pause*) White table-tops in the café where the man always sneezed. The waiter, I mean. And I thought, how odd. How odd to have a cold, a permanent cold, in the South of France. To be always blowing into handkerchiefs.

CHARLES   White.

HELEN   There were white toy horses that little children in white would pedal round the white tiling of the swimming pool. Policemen in white. White sticks in the drinks. A white piano. The trees painted white to half way up them. And the sky, white over a white sea.

CHARLES   The piano was black.

HELEN   (*Not hearing*) So I thought, how sad. How sad that none of the whiteness will be in the photographs.

CHARLES   (*To himself*) Or was it the man playing it?

HELEN   White is my favourite.

> *Pause. Then sudden, staccato hammering from behind bookcase on left wall.*

14

CHARLES At this time. Not yesterday, not the day before. Silent as a . . . like a library twelve months of the year. Then the one night, the one night, the one night.

HELEN They're putting up pictures.

CHARLES Of pop people. Of electricians with pink hair.

HELEN They had a poster of the Charioteer of Delphi. A lovely big one, a black and white one.

CHARLES Not yesterday. Not last night.

HELEN And one of a girl.

Hammering stops.

Of a girl in a muslin dress in a tree in an orchard. Slipping off the branch. In very . . . hazy colours.

CHARLES And a turkey red poster of Che, or a pig in a bobby's helmet.

HELEN That was years ago.

CHARLES I teach them. I know them.

HELEN Years ago. (*Pause*) Have you ever seen Philip's bedroom?

CHARLES (*Shortly*) No.

HELEN I wished them well. Their hands were frozen.

CHARLES The Charioteer of Delphi. The Charioteer of Delphi. It would break your heart.

Car headlights cross the room from right to left.

HELEN 'Ciao,' they said. It used to be 'See you'. Or 'So long'. And do you know what I said? I said 'Ciao-y'. And they laughed.

CHARLES The first time, the very first time, in the old museum, before they built the new one, when I came upon it — just like that, not expecting it, not expecting anything — I was ashamed. I was ashamed of my . . . shorts, and the catalogue, and of my camera. Of the camera, most of all. And of not being prepared. (*Pause*) I wiped the sun oil off my face. I felt so . . . shy. And I just . . . sat there, for an hour, listening to it.

HELEN Its big, mournful eyes.

CHARLES Not big, not mournful. Patient. Used to everything.

15

Two thousand years in the earth. Hearing the roots
... shift, and the sun teasing the wheat, or a little wind
making ... insect noises.

'Phone rings abruptly.

No, no, no.
HELEN Don't shout. Please don't shout.
CHARLES Twelve months of the year.

'Phone stops. Silence.

HELEN (*Lamely*) It's stopped.
CHARLES Philip. Try twice. No answer. They're out.

CHARLES *stands, and makes to move.*

HELEN Where are you going?
CHARLES (*Cruelly*) I have to empty my bag.

*When he reaches the 'phone, he stoops to pull out the
cord. Stands, his back to* HELEN. *She may be about to
cry.*

HELEN I understand.
CHARLES Do you?

Pause.

HELEN No.

They look at each other.

Scene 3: Eight O'Clock

As before. HELEN *is sitting on the couch.* CHARLES *is standing at the fireplace, looking into it. Car headlights cross the room from left to right.*

HELEN Shall I close the curtains?
CHARLES When have we ever closed the curtains?
HELEN I could just pull them across. (*Pause*) Or draw the blinds.
CHARLES Peeping Toms.

> *Pause. Car headlights cross the room from left to right.*

Close the curtains.
HELEN Not if you don't want to.
CHARLES I don't mind.

> *Pause.*

HELEN Did you manage?
CHARLES Yes. Am I all right?
HELEN You look . . . very handsome.
CHARLES (*Touched, awkward*) I'm . . . trying to match you.
HELEN Oh, I look . . . ordinary. (*Pause*) I didn't know whether you wanted me to . . . dress . . . or dress up.
CHARLES (*Turning to her*) I put on that tie. You remember.
HELEN No.
CHARLES No?
HELEN Of course.
CHARLES (*All pretence gone*) Neither do I.

> *They laugh a little. Silence.*

HELEN Charles?

CHARLES Hmm?

HELEN If you won't . . .

CHARLES Won't?

HELEN If you won't, or can't, speak to him . . . on the 'phone, couldn't you put . . . something on tape? Nothing very big, I mean. But something.

Pause.

CHARLES That would be . . . theatrical.

HELEN When you brought him back, you remember, from the conference in Munich, when you brought him back, and he'd been so unhappy, because he was little, I suppose, and he'd hated the food, and the smells, and the strange . . . language. You remember I'd been . . .

CHARLES Very tired.

HELEN I'd been very tired, and so you took him with you while I stayed on . . . longer, to get better.

CHARLES I gave my best paper at that conference. Not that it matters. Philip in the front row, bored to tears, legs not reaching the carpet, thin little legs; and me talking about the *pharmakos* in fifth century Athens.

HELEN I was at home waiting for you. They'd brought me home the day before. You were so cross when you found out. But I saw you coming in, getting out of the taxi with him, with Philip, and he kneeled down, on his bare knees, and kissed the gravel, he was so happy to be home.

CHARLES He was so happy to be home.

HELEN It isn't so long ago.

CHARLES It's too long ago. (*Pause*) Much too . . . really.

HELEN Just a few minutes. Something silly or personal, something intimate. (*Pause*) Perhaps not intimate. But something.

CHARLES Everything has been organised. Everything has been . . . laid out.

HELEN When you went to watch him playing cricket, the day he was hit.

CHARLES Everything has been arranged. Has been settled.

HELEN His coming from the baths with wet hair, and you

18

driving to the headmaster about it.

Car headlights cross the room from right to left.

CHARLES Instructions have been left, accounts have been . . . determined, affairs are in order.

HELEN Or the walk on the railway, along the tracks, where he walked behind you, skipping on the sleepers, and talking to himself; but everything he said was said for you. When he talked about —

CHARLES There is nothing that remains to be done.

HELEN You gave out to him for not doing his homework, but when you came down you had glue on your fingers from helping him make his Messerschmitt or his Spitfire.

CHARLES These things are imagined.

Sudden, staccato hammering from behind bookcase on left wall. A book drops off one of the shelves. Hammering stops. Silence.

None of this happened. (*Pause*) Some of it perhaps. (*Long pause*) The Messerschmitt. (*Long pause*) The Messerschmitt happened.

CHARLES kneels down beside HELEN, holds her hand in his. She is looking down at her lap.

Your poor hands.

HELEN (*Dazed*) Are they?

CHARLES When you modelled gloves —

HELEN (*This is an old exchange; they parody it.*) For two days.

CHARLES Your hands were beautiful.

HELEN Enticing?

CHARLES Very.

Car headlights cross the room from left to right.

HELEN I was your Nausicaa.

CHARLES You were my white-elbowed Nausicaa.

HELEN I was your Athene.

CHARLES You were my grey-eyed Athene.

HELEN Grey-eyed and grey-haired.

CHARLES Not grey-haired. Not then. Not later. (*Pause*) Long after. I saw your first grey hair long after. I picked it out with my thumb and my index finger, just like so. (*Gestures*) A long, delicate, warm hair. And I put it in my bureau. I put it in my diary. Between the pages. The pages for that day. Between the page for the morning, and the page for the afternoon.

HELEN (*Amused, unconvinced, hopeful*) Did you really?

CHARLES Cross my heart.

HELEN No?

CHARLES Yes.

They rub foreheads.

HELEN Yes?

Pause.

CHARLES No.

They embrace. A single hammerblow from behind bookcase on left wall, as of a nail finally sinking: a decisive thud.

Scene 4: Nine O'Clock

As before. HELEN *is sitting in the single chair beside the fireplace.* CHARLES *spends much of this scene walking in a restive fashion around the room.*

HELEN   Tell me again.
CHARLES   Again?

> *Pause.*

HELEN   Just once more.
CHARLES   But why?
HELEN   A last time.
CHARLES   But why?
HELEN   So that I can be sure.

> *Car headlights cross the room from right to left.*

CHARLES   Are you not sure?
HELEN   So that I can be . . . certain.
CHARLES   Are you not certain?
HELEN   Yes. Yes, I'm certain. But this morning . . .
CHARLES   This morning? (*He turns to look at her*)
HELEN   I watered the flowers. The spiders, and the ferns, the rubbers even. The Kaffir lily and . . . the Zebra plant.
CHARLES   A motor reflex.

> *Pause.*

HELEN   I read the newspaper. I read about oil-slicks. And yellowhammers. There was a thing . . . I was going to cut out. And I thought, how strange. How strange to be cutting out a thing about . . . repotting.
CHARLES   You want the other? The silence of the ward. And a

cubicle. In the next, a radio. A radio —

HELEN (*Mechanically: this is an old routine*) Tuned to the wrong station.

CHARLES Coughing. The coughing increasing. Footsteps. Footsteps coming faster.

HELEN Wallop, flop, wallop.

CHARLES Then silence.

Car headlights cross the room from right to left.

HELEN Would that be —

CHARLES Ammonia, iodine. (*Pause*) In the morning a stranger sweeps round the lino, empties the pot, changes the pillowcase. 'It's me as should be in the bed, you look a treat.' (*Pause*) Then silence. The noise of a tray, of bins rattling, of linen baskets. The lids of commodes. The gasps of wheelchairs. A cubicle. In the next, a radio.

HELEN Not that. Not that.

CHARLES On Tuesdays, or Wednesdays, or Thursdays, some schoolboys from the local comprehensive. School-leavers with . . .

HELEN On Wednesdays, or Thursdays . . .

CHARLES With packets of tea, with pouches of tobacco, with cartons of milk, with bars of chocolate, with *Home and Country*, with comics and colour supplements, with ritual charity.

HELEN Would that be terrible? (*She does not know*)

CHARLES Then silence. A cubicle. In the next, a radio. You stare at the stain on the ceiling above you. Like a map of Africa. You think of the countries. Their old names. The new ones. Zimbabwe, Malawi, Burkina-Faso, The Ivory Coast, Togo, Senegal. The names of the rivers. Or you stare at the stain on the wall near the window. Like a map of France.

HELEN A white map. The whole country . . . snowed in. The rain falling as snow. And I thought . . .

Car headlights cross the room from left to right.

CHARLES   Your breakfast repeats. Muesli dries into the bed-spread. Antacids leave a scum on your tongue. Plumbing clinks and tinkles. Overhead, at the window, under the bed-frame. Clinks and tinkles.

HELEN   Clunk, trickle, clunk.

CHARLES   The night-nurse props you, wipes you, speaks to you . . . as if it were hard, as if the connection were bad, and she had to shout. As if she were onto . . . Australia.

HELEN   Or you were a foreigner.

CHARLES   A foreigner. In a post-office. With a phrase-book. And trying to find a phrase.

HELEN   And the night-nurse goes back.

CHARLES   The night-nurse goes back. To a Mills and Boon novel, to a knitting pattern. Period pains. Boyfriend problems. (*Pause*) You watch them from the window as they pedal down the avenue, standing on the pedals, going (*Pause*) pell-mell. Hot-footing it back to their own world. (*Pause*) In their Garibaldi blouses . . . their suede boots.

HELEN   Pell-mell. Hot-foot.

CHARLES   From May to September the heating can't be turned off. The boilerman has tried. The pipes are too hot to be touched while the grass in the garden turns brown. (*Pause*) From September to May, they put towels on the ledges, at the sash cords, to keep the rain out.

HELEN   From May to September, September to May . . .

CHARLES   The silence. A cubicle. In the next, a radio.

Car headlights cross the room from right to left.

HELEN   If you whimper, they think you're being devious.

CHARLES   If you cry, they say that you're manipulative.

HELEN   If you complain, they tell you you're spoiled.

CHARLES   When the summer comes, they leave you sitting near the gardenias and the white chains at the edge of the lawn. The sun goes in, and comes out again. They move your chair as the sun moves. Or they forget you, and you drowse on a wooden bench, and you wake up in shadow. (*Pause*) With a chaplain walking towards you. Unsure.

HELEN　And visitors?

CHARLES　Quakers. Cranks. Community nurses. Camera teams. But the real footsteps, the ones you hear coming quickly, stop at the next cubicle, or the one after, or the one before. Then the silence.

HELEN　And Philip?

CHARLES　(*Brutally*) Philip will be bending over for the next nancyboy.

HELEN　No!

> *Sudden, staccato hammering from behind bookcase on left wall.*

CHARLES　It's not for us. For people like us.

HELEN　But what frightens me —

CHARLES　I've told you.

> *Hammering increases in tempo and loudness.*

HELEN　I can't bear —

CHARLES　People like us.

HELEN　The thought of being cut up.

CHARLES　I've told you.

HELEN　I saw what they did to my mother.

> *Hammering increases in tempo and loudness.*

CHARLES　Everything will be —

HELEN　Because they didn't know, and they had to know. It's the law. You have to know the reason. Otherwise they have to do one. They have to.

CHARLES　You must trust me.

HELEN　And that's what I'm afraid of.

> *Car headlights cross the stage from left to right, and from right to left.*

CHARLES　Leave us alone!

> HELEN *covers her face with her hands.* CHARLES *walks*

*as quickly as he can to the bookcase, and bangs it
repeatedly with both raised fists.*

Leave us alone!

Hammering ceases abruptly. Dead silence. CHARLES
*remains where he is, leaning against the bookcase,
arms raised, like a suspect being frisked.* HELEN *bends
low over her lap. Pause.*

HELEN Not the silence. (*Pause*) Not the hurting now, but the
hurting afterwards.

*Car headlights cross the room from left to right, more
slowly than before.*

Scene 5: Ten O'Clock

As before. HELEN *is seated, her head bent.* CHARLES *is still standing at the bookcase, as if staring straight through it. There is a long silence.*

CHARLES I was thinking . . . (*Pause*) Today I was thinking . . .
HELEN (*Tenderly*) When have you not been thinking?
CHARLES Not that.
HELEN What then?
CHARLES Philip.

> HELEN *looks up slowly.*

HELEN Yes?
CHARLES As a child. As a boy, I mean. I don't know. Thirteen, fourteen. Perhaps fourteen. (*Pause*) There was a power cut.
HELEN A power cut?
CHARLES And I went into him.
HELEN Where?
CHARLES He was in darkness, total darkness. Reading by torchlight. The old rubber torch. Doing his home-work, you see. Learning his Latin, his Latin verbs. (*Slowly at first and then more rapidly, ending in an urgent whisper*) I might have been loved, you might have been loved, he might have been loved —
HELEN Don't.
CHARLES She might have been loved, we might have been loved . . . .

> *Pause.*

HELEN I know. I know what you're saying. What you're trying to say.
CHARLES (*Surprised*) What am I trying to say?
HELEN I haven't the faintest.

The two stare at each other. Then they burst out laughing. After a time, the laughter subsides. A short silence. Car lights cross the room from left to right.

(*Gently*) Dimwit. (*Pause*) Name twenty nineteenth century British Prime Ministers.

CHARLES *laughs.*

(*More vigorously*) List the principal books of the Bible.
CHARLES (*To himself*) The principal books of the Bible.
HELEN And the reasons refuting them all.
CHARLES And the reasons refuting them all. Or at least . . . some of them.

Pause.

HELEN Once it was worse. It was the worst of all. You took off your clothes, and lay in the bath. At two in the morning. Sweating.
CHARLES Never.
HELEN Sweating and shivering.
CHARLES Port? Gin? Brandy?
HELEN Whiskey.
CHARLES And?
HELEN You recited the medical terms for the twenty-seven bones of the foot. Then you threw up.

They both laugh.

CHARLES Because I had to prove, you see —
HELEN That you were still intelligent, in control. In spite of being drunk. That you could still think. Think clearly, think concisely. Think, think, think. (*Pause and sadly*) You were always so . . . terrified that you wouldn't be able to think. That your mind wouldn't work. And the irony is . . . the irony is —
CHARLES Why are you doing this?
HELEN That it was me, wasn't it? Me who went in through the white gates to a white building. And you were so

27

relieved. The Angel of the Lord would pass by your doorway because it was daubed with blood.

CHARLES Why are you doing this?

HELEN (*To herself*) White gates to a white building.

CHARLES The building was cream.

> HELEN *looks closely at* CHARLES. *She begins to giggle; the giggling increases and becomes laughter. It stops suddenly. There is a long silence. Car lights cross the room from right to left, slowly.*

HELEN One time . . . one year . . . the second year or the third year, a little before I came home, they brought us down, a few of us, as far as the gate. There was a bicycle race, and the cyclists came from all over Europe. Some of them came from Eastern Europe; some of them came from Greece. They were going to pass the gate. People were clustered on both sides of the road, waiting there. (*Pause*) So many people, waiting. (*Pause*) Then the cyclists came. Dozens of them. A hundred of them. Out of nowhere. Such . . . young men. Young bodies. Their bicycles gleaming. And everyone cheered. Everyone. And I cheered too. I cheered . . . like mad. A policeman was standing beside me. He took my hand. He took my hand in his, and he said, God is good.

CHARLES Stop. Stop it. (*Pause*) Please.

> *He walks to the 'phone and stands beside it. For a time he stares fixedly at the handset; then he lifts it slowly and leaves it off the handset. Now* HELEN *looks over at him vaguely.* CHARLES *stares at her in turn. As he does so, the first notes of Allegri's* Miserere *begin to be heard, or overheard, as if coming from the room on the other side of the wall. Little by little the volume increases imperceptibly.* HELEN *and* CHARLES *remain in silence, listening intently.*

HELEN It's so sad.

CHARLES Not sad. Not sad. Something . . . to live for. Or to live by.

HELEN What is it?

Pause.

CHARLES Shhh.
HELEN They must be a lovely couple.
CHARLES Our kind of people.
HELEN What are they looking forward to as they listen?
Something quite special. Something very private.
(*Pause*) I liked her so much.

*Music rises to its crescendo, pauses, fades away. Then
silence.*

CHARLES (*Softly*) Tell me a story.
HELEN A story?
CHARLES Yes.

Pause.

HELEN There was a boy . . . there was a girl. They were lovers.
(*Pause*) The boy took the girl to Greece. In Athens,
they went to the first hotel they could find. From their
bedroom window they could see the Acropolis rear-
ing over the rooftops. They dumped their suitcase and
ran through the streets until they reached it. And then
they sat there, under a small tree, until the sun set and
the place closed. (*Pause*) The boy couldn't remember
the name of the hotel they were staying in. Nor could
she. All they had to guide them was their room key
with the number seven written on it. (*A little laugh*)
They found it . . . five hours later. (*Long pause*) Later
that night they made love, the boy and the girl. Little
flies danced on the ceiling; the door of the wardrobe
creaked in the breeze from the street. (*Pause*) And after
they had made love, the girl went to the bathroom and
lay on the floor, on her back, on a marble floor, and
lifted her legs up over her head so that none of him
would leak out of her. She wanted him so much to stay
inside her . . . him and his child.

She sits in a sort of trance, staring into the middle distance. Then she rouses herself and turns to look at CHARLES.

Come here. Come here to me.

CHARLES *walks to where she's sitting, kneels in front of her. She strokes his hair and draws his head down onto her lap.*

But I keep forgetting, don't I? I keep forgetting we're all children. Some of us with stubble, some of us with stretchmarks. (*Pause*) All of us children.

Scene 6: Eleven O'Clock

As before. HELEN *and* CHARLES *are seated. A ship's decanter stands on a small stem table between the couch and the fireplace.*

CHARLES Do you want this chair?
HELEN But that's your chair.
CHARLES It might be more comfortable.
HELEN (*Shyly*) I'm fine.

> *Pause.*

CHARLES Helen.

> *Helen looks at him.*

CHARLES No matter.
HELEN Tell me.
CHARLES It would be . . . silly.

> *Pause.*

HELEN Is it time?
CHARLES Nearly.

> *Pause. Car headlights cross the room from right to left.*

There was a man. He had a shop, a grocery shop.
HELEN And?
CHARLES Nicotine stains along the length of his finger. When he smoked, the palps of his fingers turned . . . white.
HELEN When he inhaled.
CHARLES He gave you his sugar ration. During the war. Every week. Week in, week out. His sugar ration.
HELEN Because I was pregnant.
CHARLES Because you were beautiful.

HELEN Worn out and pregnant.
CHARLES 'Sweets for the sweet,' he'd say. A man who couldn't write. 'Sweets for the sweet.'

Pause.

HELEN I had a craving for sugar.
CHARLES Because you were beautiful.

Pause.

HELEN Is it time yet?
CHARLES Nearly.
HELEN I think it's time.
CHARLES The first night we danced, perhaps the second, you kicked off your shoes. And you danced barefoot. (*Pause*) Barefoot on the walnut floor of a ballroom.
HELEN It was the second.
CHARLES Everybody stopped dancing, just to watch you. Not one other couple came onto the floor. Not one.
HELEN One or two perhaps.
CHARLES People stood looking. And after, when it was over, they clapped you, the barefoot dancer. The soles of your feet were black from the dance-floor. (*Pause*) Black through your nylons.
HELEN (*Gently*) It must be time.

Pause.

CHARLES From our best glasses.
HELEN The best of them.
CHARLES Like Greeks.
HELEN Like Romans.
CHARLES And into the fireplace with them.
HELEN Like Russians.
CHARLES Like Russians.

Pause. CHARLES *hums. Stops, hums a different tune. Stops.*

The mind.

HELEN (*Gently*) Don't.

CHARLES What was that chap's name? And the tune? An Irish name, an American tune. And the black soles of your feet.

Pause. Hesitant knocking at door.

Don't.

HELEN *stirs as if to stand.* CHARLES *shakes his head softly. Knocking resumes, a little louder, more confident.*

O'Connor? O'Conaher?

Pause. Another knock. Car headlights cross the room from right to left.

The Moon Over Tuscany?

Pause. The sound of paper being slid under the door.

Sweets for the sweet. One tooth in his head. He could crack an apple with his gums.

CHARLES *stands, walks about the room, putting out the two standard lights.*

HELEN But —

CHARLES (*Gently*) No matter. (*Pause*) You couldn't eat on your own. You know. They'd have to keep a nurse there. In case you choked on a piece of gristle. Or a runner bean.

CHARLES *stoops at the door, picks up a folded note, walks back to the fireplace.*

HELEN (*Dazed*) Philip?

CHARLES In the museum, before they built the new one, there was a . . . guard. He had to sit all day in the room with the Charioteer. He was . . . worn-out. (*Pause*) Worn-out. (*Pause*) Watery eyes . . . and such sad hands.

HELEN I feel strange.

CHARLES *opens the note, reads it.*

CHARLES It says there will be no more . . . noise. (*Pause*) No more hammering. We won't have any reason . . . to complain. (*Pause*) There are two little matchstick figures holding a banner with (*Pause*) the word 'Sorry' written on it.

HELEN And tired. Suddenly.

CHARLES I get the faces mixed up. The man with the sugar ration, and then the guard.

CHARLES *hums. Stops.*

The mind plays tricks.

He brings from the mantel two elegant stem glasses.

Like two Greeks.

HELEN I —

CHARLES Yes?

HELEN Never mind.

CHARLES Tell me. (*Pause*) Tell me.

HELEN May I close the curtains? Would that be all right?

Pause. Car headlights cross the room from left to right. HELEN *and* CHARLES *sit together, holding hands.*

CHARLES That would be all right. (*Pause*) That would be fine.

Curtain

ENTRANCE

Scene 1: Six O'Clock

The empty living room of an apartment in a period town-house. Several tea-chests, stamped with serial numbers and the names of foreign cities, are stacked in a sort of pyramid in the middle of the room. Otherwise the place is bare. Bandage marks on the walls where previous tenants had hung pictures. A door at rere; another at left back-stage. Windows to be imagined at front stage where the curtains open and close.

HELEN is kneeling in front of the tea-chests, removing small items wrapped in newspaper. Loose newsprint pages all round her. CHARLES is sitting on a tea-chest, his back to her, lifting books singly and in stacks from another container. From time to time, he chooses a volume, leafs through it, is absorbed. HELEN unwinds a paper package like an onion, letting the crumpled sheets lie where they fall. At last, the mystery is revealed: one china cup. She sets it down beside two others near her. Holds up another parcelled object. Shakes it at her ear. CHARLES looks back at her.

HELEN I think I've found it.
CHARLES What?
HELEN Guess.
CHARLES Bathroomy?
HELEN Cold.
CHARLES Bedroomy?
HELEN No.
CHARLES Kitcheny?
HELEN Warmer.
CHARLES (*Looks at the large parcel critically*) An egg-cup.
HELEN A ramekin for paté.
CHARLES A ramekin for paté.

She unwraps it rapidly. CHARLES *returns to his book.*
HELEN *produces a ramekin and holds it up.*

HELEN   Presto. I know where everything is. (*This delights her*)
        The only thing I'm missing so far . . .

CHARLES   (*Smells the book he's holding*) I should have cleaned
        these tea-chests out.

HELEN   (*Not hearing*) . . . is the blue pastry dish.

CHARLES   (*Irritated*) My Sophocles stinks of tea.

HELEN   (*Not hearing*) With the crack on the underneath of it.

CHARLES   I wouldn't mind coffee.

HELEN   (*Thoughtfully*) But you can hardly see the crack.

Pause.

CHARLES   (*To himself*) Tomorrow.

HELEN   Tomorrow what?

CHARLES   The lights. Lighting. Electricity.

HELEN   Doesn't matter.

CHARLES   First thing tomorrow.

HELEN   It's fun.

CHARLES   Too late tonight.

HELEN   It's an adventure.

CHARLES   (*Looks at her*) This is not the scouts.

HELEN   We can get candles.

CHARLES   Where will we get candles?

HELEN   (*Patiently*) From a church, Hedgehog.

Pause.

CHARLES   (*Making an effort*) You do like it?

HELEN   (*Tartly*) No, I hate it. I took one look at it and I thought
        to myself, Yuk. I hate it so much I'm half way through
        my second tea-chest while you sit there reading.

CHARLES   (*Walking about*) It is rather nice. (*Pause*) A bit bare.

HELEN   Spacious.

CHARLES   And a bit drafty.

HELEN   Airy.

CHARLES   But it's different.

HELEN   Very.

Pause.

CHARLES It's us.

HELEN (*Tenderly*) Us.

CHARLES And tomorrow the lights. Tomorrow and tomorrow and tomorrow.

HELEN (*Excited*) Hundreds of tomorrows. Hundreds. (*Pause*) Tomorrow I'm going to paint.

CHARLES She's going to paint.

HELEN Everything white. Vanilla white. To make it brighter. To bring it up. The smell of paint everywhere.

CHARLES Not on my books.

HELEN Plus —

CHARLES They stink enough already.

HELEN Plus I'm going to invite the couple next door. For tea and scones.

CHARLES They know we're not quite kosher.

HELEN (*Defensive*) They couldn't care less, I'm sure. You've the silliest notions. (*Pause*) I thought she was sweet. She looked . . . wistful.

CHARLES (*Ruminant*) She must have been stunning. That bone-structure. And the most beautiful hands. (*Spreads his, examines them*) But those cross, suspicious eyes.

HELEN I thought she was —

CHARLES Rather nice, to be honest.

HELEN Rather nice, to be honest.

Pause.

CHARLES When did Stephen say he was coming?

HELEN Do you know . . . I was almost hoping that —

CHARLES (*Teasing*) Yes?

HELEN I love Stephen, of course.

CHARLES But?

HELEN That tonight . . . just tonight. That he wouldn't come. Because —

CHARLES Because?

HELEN Because. (*She is embarrassed*)

In response to whatever this may mean, CHARLES

moves towards HELEN — *as if breaking his orbit around her* — *and starts rummaging in a tea-chest.*

CHARLES Where's Dimwit?
HELEN I put him with Frolic.
CHARLES Where the devil are they?

> CHARLES *peers down into the tea-chest, sees what he's looking for, smiles. In a baby voice, then:*

Hello, Dimwit.
HELEN Is Frolic with him?
CHARLES (*Baby voice*) They is fast asleep. (*He reaches in*)
HELEN Not yet. (*She holds up a* God Bless Our Home *sign*) Put this up first.
CHARLES (*Normal voice*) No. (*Pause*) Never.
HELEN Please.
CHARLES Never.
HELEN Who packed your books for you?

> *Pause.*

CHARLES Where?

> HELEN *points like a child* — *she is playing home* — *at the wall on right.* CHARLES *takes hammer and nail from top of tea-chest, trudges to wall. He is playacting too.*

HELEN (*Rewarding him*) And you can put up that other awful thing if you want.

> *She reaches forward on her hunkers to a parcelled object, and brandishes it. Charles rounds on her: the playacting is over.*

CHARLES Don't touch that. (*Pause*) That goes over my desk. When I'm ready.

> HELEN *replaces it.* CHARLES *turns to wall, holds nail against it, wallops in the nail with short precise strokes.*

Hangs sign, straightens it, stands back.

It comes down when we have people in.
HELEN And what if Stephen arrives?

For answer, CHARLES *swings a heavy tea-chest off the ground onto another one, blocking off the view of the sign.*

(*Alarmed*) Mind your back. You'll be crippled when you're fifty.
CHARLES (*Proud of his strength*) I'll never be fifty.
HELEN Don't say that.
CHARLES (*Looks at her*) I'll live to be a hundred.
HELEN Stop it.
CHARLES (*Amused*) A hundred and one?
HELEN (*With a kind of desolate urgency*) That doesn't give us long enough.

They look at each other. The chime of a clock heard offstage.

Scene 2: Seven O'Clock

As before. HELEN *is seated at a tea-chest, writing.* CHARLES *at window, looking towards the audience.*

CHARLES You know?

HELEN Wait.

CHARLES (*As if deciding*) I can write in here.

HELEN Be with you.

CHARLES (*Looking up*) The tall ceiling. I always work best where the ceilings are tall. Always. (*Pause*) Tomorrow I'm going to finish that essay. Finally. Full stop. Otherwise it would just go on, wouldn't it? (*Pause*) I'm going to dot my i's tomorrow. Let the ink dry. But already . . . already I can see another essay coming out of it. (*Pause*) Fresh growth.

HELEN (*Not hearing*) That's wonderful.

CHARLES This time on the tragic plays. Just the tragic ones. (*Turns to Helen*) Do you know the Greek word 'eleos' means two things?

HELEN (*Not hearing*) That's marvellous.

CHARLES It means pity. Yes. Fine. Why not? Any fool knows that. But (*He lifts his finger*) it also means . . . a butcher's table. (*Excited*) You see the connection?

HELEN (*Looks at him vaguely*) But I can't get anything in until the electricity comes on.

CHARLES (*Stares at her*) I might as well talk to the wall.

HELEN (*Brightly*) The basics. (*Lists them rapidly*) Bread, butter, milk, cheese, tea, sugar, marmalade. (*Pause; thinks*) Kitchen foil. (*Remembers*) Eggs.

CHARLES I am making a revolutionary connection. I am having an insight. It disproves everybody.

HELEN (*Not hearing*) It only becomes home when you cook in it. When you come into it, and you smell your own smells. Home smells.

CHARLES (*Smells*) Tea.

HELEN   You have to talk to it. (*Looks around her*) You have to
        talk to a new space. You must say to it, 'I won't be any
        trouble. I shall be very quiet. Promise'. (*Pause*) When
        it listens, you must listen back. Only harder.

> CHARLES *starts to unwrap the parcel* HELEN *picked up
> earlier. He unwinds it like a turban to reveal — with a
> dramatic flourish — a scale copy of the death-mask of
> Agamemnon, which he bears before him, his two hands
> held out, like a votive offering, as he walks to the left
> wall where he holds it at the height of a man, and
> studies it intensely.*

        (*Writing again*) What did you say about the butcher's?
CHARLES I said I could write in here.
HELEN   (*Looks up at him, pleased*) You think so?
CHARLES I think so. With my pen in hand. Singlehandedly.
HELEN   Battle-stations!
CHARLES Banzai!

> HELEN *claps madly.*

        (*Turning from wall, placing death-mask down*) The
        whole place is . . . propitious. The tall ceilings. The
        high windows. And it struck me, you know, it struck
        me that a year ago, one year to the day —
HELEN   (*Pleased by this*) I know.
CHARLES We went to the Greek Exhibition.
HELEN   (*Disappointed*) I thought it was the day we went —
CHARLES For the first time. Or was it the second?
HELEN   (*Conceding*) I remember.
CHARLES Only a starter, of course. A taste. It's all ahead of us.
HELEN   It was a lovely day.
CHARLES That calyx of Apollo pouring a libation. (*He imitates the
        gesture*) Five hundred years before the birth of Christ.
        (*Pause*) Pouring.
HELEN   And the bits and pieces.
CHARLES (*Sitting on tea-chest*) The bits and pieces?
HELEN   (*Abashed*) Of pottery.
CHARLES Pottery?

HELEN (*Remembering*) Where they scribbled messages. You know. 'Demosthenes, I lost the key to the back door. See you anon' . . . or (*Lamely, feeling Charles's whimsy*) 'Plato, your mother was worried. Where are you? Father'. (*Pause*) I could see them somehow.

CHARLES (*Taking up her shopping list and reading it to himself*) Perhaps in the next millennium when our mutant great-great-greats are staring into exhibition cases at a touring show on Jupiter —

> HELEN *makes a grab at the slip of paper;* CHARLES *holds it above his head.*

They'll have to reconstruct our culture from a shopping list like this. The works of the philos⌣phers will be anybody's guess. Schools of jellyfish will drift in the currents above the courtyards of Versailles; turtles will lay their eggs in the sands of the British Museum —

> HELEN *finally snatches it from him. Her mood is undecided.*

But back on Jupiter, that elusive papyrus has at last been broken. Relays of dons have been working at it for generations.

HELEN (*Reading her list*) I forgot the pound of sausages and a packet of streaky rashers.

CHARLES (*With bravado*) Ladies and gentlemen, I give you a pound of sausages and a packet of streaky rashers.

> HELEN *doesn't respond. Dead silence.* CHARLES *a little uneasy for a moment. Turns to the window, hands in pockets. Looks over his shoulder at* HELEN.

(*Gently*) Do you know?

HELEN Hmm?

CHARLES I'll take you there some day.

HELEN (*She is quite preoccupied*) Where?

CHARLES You know.

HELEN   (*Coming to*) To the Peloponnese. (*She pronounces this very deliberately*)

CHARLES   (*Pleased*) To the Peloponnese. And after that, I'll whisk you —

HELEN   To the island of Delos.

CHARLES   To the island of Delos.

HELEN   And you'll carry me to the top of Mount Cynthnos.

CHARLES   Where the lizards glide like fish through the scutch grass.

HELEN   I hate lizards.

CHARLES   And after that, after that, I'll take you —

HELEN   (*Humouring him*) With one big rucksack and one lickle one —

CHARLES   Side by side, hand in hand, to the loveliest thing of all. One night, when the moon is full, et cetera, et cetera . . . (*He waves his hand about*)

HELEN   When the museum's empty.

CHARLES   His eyes staring into the most unimaginable distances. His hands held out. The noise of the crowd a blue shimmer around him: not seen.

HELEN   The Charioteer of Delphi.

CHARLES   Sad and silent.

HELEN   Silent and sad.

> CHARLES *has been slowly assuming the stiff, remote posture of the Charioteer. Now he freezes, a facsimile of the statue.* HELEN *dislikes this. She watches a moment, then moves towards him.*

Charles, stop. (*He doesn't respond*) Stop.

> *She slaps him. He looks at her, grins, walks to a tea-chest, searches among it, draws out two koala glove-puppets, one of which he slips onto his left hand.* HELEN *puts the other on her hand. When they talk, it is in baby accents.*

CHARLES   How is you, Frolic?

HELEN   I is well, Dimwit. Is you happy?

CHARLES *kneels down in front of* HELEN, *and puts his gloved hand on her lap near the other puppet.*

CHARLES Yuss, I is. Does you like your new koala nest?
HELEN Oh, it is luverly. It is the mostest nicest koalest nest I have ever seed.

Pause. HELEN *and* CHARLES *dance the puppets about in her lap. Then their gloved hands entwine; the puppets embrace.*

Dimwit?
CHARLES Yuss, Frolic?
HELEN What special thing is going to happen tonights? Tell Frolic.

Long pause. CHARLES *stands, strips the puppet from his hand. Resumes normal voice.*

CHARLES Bedtime for Dimwit. (*Throws the puppet aside*)
HELEN Poor Dimwit. Poor, poor —
CHARLES Stop it. (*Pause*) Stop.
HELEN (*Her normal voice*) You won't talk to me.

Pause.

CHARLES I should go and get candles. It'll be dark soon.
HELEN We never talk about the things that matter.
CHARLES And Stephen may come.
HELEN What are we doing here? What are we entering into? And where is it going to lead us?
CHARLES (*Scooping up hammer and nail*) And I'll take you to Tiryns.
HELEN Why have we come here?
CHARLES Then to Mycenae.
HELEN What is going to happen here?
CHARLES And then to the theatre of Epidauros. (*Stands at wall, bangs in nail*)
HELEN Talk to me.
CHARLES (*Taking up death-mask to hang it*) Epidauros is beauti-

ful. You haven't lived till you've seen Epidauros. In the summer, the sun lies on your back like an arm round your shoulder: winter, it snows. (*He is talking rapidly now*) We'll go in the winter. If there's no snow, we'll order some. (*More quietly, turning to her*) I want to be with you when you see it. I want to look at you as you look at it. Your face will light up. (*Gently*) My little Penelope.

HELEN Sod Penelope. I don't want to be Penelope.

CHARLES I can quite see why. Buttonholed by Romeos. Fending 'em off, six at a time, with a swipe of your thimble.

HELEN You know what I want.

CHARLES You are my Helen of Troy.

HELEN I don't want to be Helen of Troy. (*Pause*) I want you to be you and I want me to be me.

Long pause. They look at each other.

Charles and Helen.

Pause.

CHARLES Helen and Charles.

The chime of a clock heard offstage.

Scene 3: Eight O'Clock

CHARLES *seated at left;* HELEN *rooting among the contents of a tea-chest. At left a largish mirror leaning against wall. By now, the room has lost its bare look. But the adornments serve only to emphasise a sense of fragility rather than of cosiness. Outside, it is getting dark. Stage-lights a little lower.*

HELEN (*Holding up a piece of paper*) And this?

CHARLES I can't possibly imagine.

HELEN The programme from *The Barber of Seville*.

CHARLES (*Incredulous*) That too?

HELEN (*Rummaging*) There's more.

CHARLES You keep everything?

HELEN It helps me . . . to know where I am. (*Looks into tea-chest again*)

CHARLES I wish you wouldn't keep . . . fishing into that box. It makes me feel like an archaeologist. Or a grave-robber. I feel I should be in khaki, with a torch.

HELEN (*Not hearing*) Why did I save these bus-tickets? Think.

CHARLES It's like the Valley of the Kings in here. (*Runs his finger along wall, examines the tip of it*)

HELEN You know? (*Pause;* CHARLES *looks at her*) This room has been waiting for us. (*Pause*) It's been lonely. I think it's been crying.

CHARLES Just so long as the walls don't weep.

HELEN I think it remembers us. I recognise this room. (*Pause*) Perhaps I was here in a previous existence, as a scullery maid. Or a governess from Dieppe. (CHARLES *stares at her; she becomes brisk again*) I hope Stephen won't come tonight. It was kind of him to offer, I see that. But the first night is . . . hidden away, somehow. And I'm glad there's no power. I don't know why. (*Pause.* HELEN *holds something up*) And this?

CHARLES Tell me, tell me.

HELEN The menu card from the first restaurant you brought me to. The first of the four.

CHARLES Morbid. Storing fossils. Always staring back. You'll get tunnel vision.

HELEN (*Looking at the menu card*) What was the first thing you noticed about me? The very first thing.

CHARLES Your teeth. Very strong teeth.

HELEN Don't tease me.

CHARLES And the way you said 'faute de mieux'. Wrong, of course, but charming.

HELEN Tell me truly.

Pause.

CHARLES Your bone structure.

Pause.

HELEN I was drawn to you because you were dressed in corduroy. I've always found corduroy so . . . trust-worthy.

CHARLES And what if I'd been wearing houndstooth? Or tweed?

HELEN (*Simply*) I'd never have noticed you. (*Lightly*) Or I would have spurned your advances.

CHARLES I shall always wear corduroy.

HELEN My bone structure has no other plans.

Pause.

CHARLES (*Standing*) It would seem that our relationship has been brought about by a mysterious conjunction of local tailor and master anatomist.

HELEN The man next door was wearing corduroy. (*Pause*) He looked so . . . distinguished.

CHARLES He looked defeated. He looked like Death.

HELEN I thought he was sweet. (*Pause*) Will you be that patrician when we're great grandparents?

CHARLES *moves to* HELEN, *sits on a tea-chest beside*

her, looks into the slanted mirror against the wall; she is kneeling next to him, her head at shoulder level; she looks away into the mirror too.

CHARLES   I shall be emphysemic, a snarling misanthrope with a face like the mummified Rameses. I'll lurk in dark corners masticating sodium pills for my heart murmur, and wander about the West End with my flies undone. But you will still love me because I shall be armatured from throat to ankle in the finest of —

HELEN   (*Savouring it*) Non-crumple needle corduroy.

CHARLES   You'll be bald, palsied, your eyes as sad as a Capuchin monkey's. Night after night you'll sit by the wireless chewing banana sandwiches as your gums soften with scurvy and your molars loosen. I'll have to strain your fillings from the bathwater with a gold-pan. (*Pause*) But I shall still love you because of an accident of anatomy which makes so fine an art out of bare bones. (*Caresses the back of her head*) From the refinements of your styloid process and your lambdoidal suture to (*Traces the bone above and below her mouth*) the felicities of your maxilla and your mandible.

Pause.

HELEN   Is that a proposal?
CHARLES   Would it do?
HELEN   It might.

Long pause. CHARLES *stands, straightens, hands in pockets, looks through window.* HELEN *watches him.*

CHARLES   Quiet.
HELEN   Yes.
CHARLES   Very quiet.
HELEN   As quiet as white.

Pause.

CHARLES   I wonder what the people next door are thinking.

Perhaps they think we're bad news. A regrettable element. (*Pause*) Perhaps they have a stethoscope pressed to the wall. (*Waves at the wall*) Perhaps they're voyeurs.

HELEN I keep thinking, you know, that it's so . . . strange. Lives are going on all round us. Above and below, to each side: men and women, women and men. Lives that make no noise. (*Pause*) We'll be happy here.

CHARLES And I can write. (*Looks at her, looks away quickly*) You have your cry-look. Please don't. The least little thing sets you off. It's not fair. It's manipulative. (*Pause*) I can't cope with your cry-look.

HELEN Charles?

> *Pause.*

What would you do if I had a child?

CHARLES (*Thinks about this*) I would take out a life-insurance policy.

HELEN What kind of a child would we have?

CHARLES And I'd put his name down. One has to look ahead.

HELEN If we were very close tonight, we might begin a child. Isn't that the strangest thought?

CHARLES Dimwit could be his godfather, and Frolic his maiden aunt.

HELEN Here among the tea-chests. It's so silly and terrifying.

CHARLES Tell him the stories I was told. The Black Forest. Crocodile Croak and Gorilla the Bloody. (*Thinks*) Start on the Greeks a little later.

HELEN Talk to me.

CHARLES What shall we talk about?

> *He swings around. Pause.* HELEN *starts removing clothes from a tea-chest. Folded shirts, etc.*

HELEN Gregory is a lovely name.

CHARLES Grex, gregis, a flock. (*Pause*) No. Something less . . . sheepish. I like Alexander. A trifle grandiose, perhaps.

HELEN (*Fondly*) A trifle.

CHARLES His daddy then.
  HELEN Whose daddy?
CHARLES Lover of horses. Like my grandfather.
  HELEN Who?
CHARLES Philippos. Philip of Macedon.
  HELEN Philip is nice.

> *Pause. Helen presses one of Charles's shirts to her face, and inhales deeply.*

CHARLES Are you crying? (*Alarmed*)
  HELEN (*Looks at him*) I love your smells. (*Pause, while he looks at her uncertainly*) Come here to me.

> *The chime of a clock heard offstage.*

Scene 4: Nine O'Clock

CHARLES *kneeling at right among several columns of books. A broken book-case lies on its back in front of him. He is trying to reassemble it. A hammer and nails lie about; for the moment, though, he's busy aligning sections of wood. He might even at moments resemble an undertaker.* HELEN *enters from room at left, her sleeves rolled to her elbows. It is darker than the last scene.*

CHARLES (*Not looking*) Have you seen my copy of Dodds on the Irrational?

HELEN No, I haven't seen your copy of Dodds on the Irrational.

CHARLES I know I packed it.

HELEN (*Starts rubbing her back against door jamb*) Can that not wait?

CHARLES I start feeling at home when my books are unpacked. And I thought I put Dodds with the other D's. You were helping me with them.

HELEN I sensed that was coming.

CHARLES I'm not accusing you. (*Pause*) I might have packed it with the I's.

HELEN The I's?

CHARLES Irrational. (*Pause*) But I wouldn't have done that.

HELEN (*Rubbing her back against the door jamb*) You can never reach the itch with your hands. It's almost a law: the itch is always an inch beyond you. (*Picks a book from a column at her feet and moves it up and down behind her back*) Now I have it.

CHARLES Dodds?

HELEN Oh, that's so nice.

> CHARLES *leans over, looks at the column she took the book from.*

CHARLES P. (*Amused*) You're using Plato to scratch yourself.

HELEN I've finally found a use for him.
CHARLES (*Offers her a large bound volume*) You can get farther down with this one.
HELEN (*Throws the book down*) Stop thinking I'm a fool.
CHARLES (*Takes it up carefully, sets it aside*) It is you who say it.

Pause.

HELEN (*Kicks at a column of books and scatters them*) Their own authors would wince at the way you use them.
CHARLES What are you saying?
HELEN You use them as . . . sandbags. Sandbags!
CHARLES (*Standing*) You resent them.
HELEN (*Tired*) No, I don't. I don't resent them.
CHARLES (*Kicking other columns of books and toppling them*) Away with them so! Away with them.
HELEN (*Scuffling with Charles, trying to stop him*) Stop it, stop it.
CHARLES (*Fiercely*) Stop it, we'll be heard.

Dead silence. They kneel down, facing each other. Long pause.

Poor Frolic.
HELEN Poor, sad Dimwit.
CHARLES Nasty books.
HELEN You need your books. I understand that.
CHARLES I hate them. I use them to shut life out.
HELEN No, you don't. You use them to let light in.
CHARLES I'd like to go somewhere they could never find me.
HELEN You'd be lost without them.
CHARLES Ear-mufflers.
HELEN Hearing-aids.
CHARLES Foot-warmers.
HELEN Snow-shoes.
CHARLES Eye-patches.
HELEN (*Pause*) I'll think of something.

They laugh.

CHARLES Has your itch gone?

HELEN Go back to your books.

CHARLES No.

HELEN (*Surprised*) No?

CHARLES Yes.

HELEN (*Unsure*) Yes or no?

CHARLES Yes and no.

> *They hug each other, then sit back to back on the floor,
> leaning against each other.*

HELEN Let's get married.

CHARLES In like a shot.

HELEN The two of us.

CHARLES When a man's down.

HELEN Very quietly.

CHARLES Seize the day.

HELEN I love you.

CHARLES And that's why.

HELEN Why what?

CHARLES Why marriage might be the best thing for Helen and Charles.

HELEN Might?

CHARLES If ever a marriage was made in Heaven —

HELEN But that's the point, little hedgehog. Marriages have to be made on earth. And out of it. Out of our own . . . buried treasure.

CHARLES Half a dozen tea-chests.

HELEN Tea-chests are a sort of treasure-chest. In a way. In their own way. (*Pause*) I wish you could love me with a little less subtlety. I wish you could love me . . . in a stupid way. There's nothing wrong with milk on the doorstep, and the smell of toast on a pair of pyjamas. Nothing at all.

CHARLES For people like us?

HELEN People like us are like people everywhere.

CHARLES You want to end up like the people next door?

HELEN Would that be terrible?

CHARLES (*Teasing*) Cuttlefish in a budgie cage. Sea-shells for ashtrays. The works of Charles Dickens. (*Pause*) Rows of them.

HELEN These are good things.

CHARLES Each morning you clean out the ashes and start again.

HELEN Good things.

Pause.

CHARLES (*Shifts position, kneels at the book-case, picks up hammer*) I know. I know they are. (*Examines wood*) Couldn't take it. The journey. Too fragile. Fell apart. (*Pause; he begins to drive a nail in*) I saw my parents. I saw them. Thirty-seven years they were thick as thieves. No acrimony, no dissension, no voices raised. (*Pause*) Not a sound.

HELEN They were perfectly happy.

CHARLES They were perfect strangers. My father never knew that my mother had a prolapse problem. My mother never knew that my father wore a false tooth. They undressed away from each other, behind brown dressing gowns. Every morning they sat across the table from each other and they listened to the wireless tell them about people they cared nothing for, places they never wanted to visit, events that failed even to brush them in passing. (*Stops what he's doing, looks up*) Had a poinsettia for years. Never once reddened. They'd look at it, the green leaves. Not a blush on them. 'Maybe next year.' (*Pause*) When we came from the graveyard, my father and I, he stood there underneath his umbrella. I can see him, staring down at the double knot in his shoelace, and then looking at me, and saying —

HELEN Well, well.

CHARLES Well, well. (*Long pause*) I'll tell you what breaks a man. What grinds him down into a fine dust. Flake by flake, molecule by molecule, till his face is worn away like the face of a statue on a public building. It's not an act of God, a stroke of fate, a fluke of misfortune. None of those things. A man can cope with a child in coma, a house in flames, a woman in mourning. A dead elm crashes through his rafters. It's nothing. A cell bursts at the back of his skull, and half of his body goes into hiding. Nothing. His chief concern, his private vanity, the very centre of his life turns to a dirty fungus in the palms of his hands. Does he break down? Does he go under? (*Pause*) He perfects a style; he takes it on the chin.

HELEN He wakes up to find it's been snowing all night.

CHARLES Catastrophe and crisis are his meat and potatoes. He wolfs them down. He's flush again. His poinsettias redden. (*Pause*) But seven things defeat him. Seven things turn his life into a grey area, a tundra that goes on and on and on. (*Starts hammering loudly, one hammerblow to a word*) Monday. Tuesday. Wednesday. Thursday. Friday. Saturday. Sunday.

Frenzied counter-hammering on the other side of the wall. CHARLES *stops dead; he and* HELEN *stare fixedly at the wall. Then total silence. The chime of a clock heard offstage.*

Scene 5: Ten O'Clock

HELEN *is alone. The room is gradually darkening. The last of the sun glitters on the surface of the mirror before which she is kneeling, studying herself. She experiments with a number of facial expressions: alluring, coquettish, pensive by turns. Stops, smiles, combs out her hair, humming a tune. Picks up a bottle of perfume, scatters some on her hand, then runs her fingers along her throat and behind her ears. Opens top buttons of her blouse, hesitates, listens. A pause. Raises her right arm, smells her armpit; does the same for the other arm; then pulls at the slack of her blouse on either side to cool herself. Picks up a tin of powder, waits, listens, holds out the collar of her blouse and tips in a generous cloud of talcum. Closes blouse, brushes her fingers clean along her skirt, stands up, looks around room, steps out of her shoes, stoops at a tea-chest, removes a folded multi-coloured bedspread, shakes it out, lies it on floor, spreads and smooths it. Bends to pick up shoes, hears noise at door, glances towards it, sits quickly, pretends to be absorbed in a book or magazine which she leafs through.* CHARLES *enters, wearing a jacket, holding a brown paper bag. Stands looking at her.*

CHARLES Hasn't come yet?
HELEN (*Vexed*) No, he hasn't.

> *Pause.* CHARLES *puts bag down, removes jacket.*

You got some?
CHARLES I have everything we need.
HELEN I knew the church would be open.
CHARLES (*Coming to her with bag*) I stand corrected. (*Pause. He smells something, can't be sure what*) I paid my respects at every shrine.
HELEN And you left money?
CHARLES Madam, in all things I obey you. (*He kneels at side of bedspread, looks at it for a moment, shakes out bag. About twenty small white candles tumble out*) Voilà.

HELEN (*Laughing*) Three or four would have done. You're a hedgehog.

CHARLES Where would one be without the Church?

HELEN In total darkness in just about an hour.

CHARLES I came like a thief in the night.

HELEN You said you paid.

CHARLES And so I did. An old woman kept one eye on me the whole time I was there. I could feel her tracking me like a periscope as I looted the transepts. So I fed my coins in very ostentatiously. (*Imitates the gesture*) After a while the Cyclops resumed her supplications.

HELEN (*Sorting them*) There's enough for a siege.

CHARLES It would seem that Saint Dominic has won the hearts of the faithful. His colleagues couldn't hold a candle to him. The lights at his shrine made a huge splash. (*Pause*) Which made me wonder — (*Stops, lifts a candle, shakes his head*) — that one's broken — which made me wonder why he wore so doleful an expression on his rather fine face. A sort of dromedary look.

HELEN Now we need saucers.

CHARLES But I struck it rich at the sanctuary of one Martin de Porres, coloured, before whom two or three woebegone squibs were preparing for their final journey.

HELEN Poor man.

CHARLES He had a whimsical look. I suspect he was an ironist who understood fashion.

> *Pause.* HELEN *and* CHARLES *look at the candles, then at each other.* CHARLES *begins to sniff the air like a bloodhound. She smiles at him.*

HELEN Placet?

CHARLES Placet. (*Long pause*) Vivamus atque amemus.

> *As they look at each other, the first strains of an adagio passage from Mahler's* Das Lied Von Der Erde *begin to be heard, or overheard, as if coming from the room on the other side of the wall at right. Both of them stare at the wall. Little by little the volume increases imperceptibly, but it never becomes intrusive or definite.*

CHARLES *stands, walks towards wall, stops, looks back at* HELEN. *She begins to move her arms as if conducting the music.* CHARLES *does likewise in a slow and stately fashion. He isn't playacting; he is affected, entranced.*

HELEN   It's so sad.

CHARLES   (*Continues conducting in dumbshow, following the music more and more precisely until, at a certain point, he begins to lead it*) You could die listening to it.

HELEN   What is it?

Pause.

CHARLES   It is the music of the spheres.

HELEN   (*Recognising it*) It's *The Song of the Earth.*

CHARLES   (*Not hearing*) Shhh.

HELEN   They must be a lovely couple.

CHARLES   Our kind of people. (*He goes on conducting*)

HELEN   We should write them a note. (*Pause*) About the noise we made. (*Pause*) What are they remembering as they listen? Something quite special. Something very private. (*Pause*) I liked her so much. (*Emphatically*) 'How are you?' she said, 'How are you?'

Music rises to its crescendo, pauses.

CHARLES   (*Bows to wall*) Strange how the sound carries. No cavities.

HELEN   Charles? (*Pause; he doesn't answer*) If Stephen should come, don't answer. Not tonight. Please.

CHARLES   (*Looks at her*) I can't pretend we're not here.

HELEN   We won't make a sound. We'll wait till his footsteps go away. He'll never know.

CHARLES   (*Doubtfully*) You'll sneeze, and give the game away.

HELEN   I won't even breathe. I won't move a muscle.

CHARLES   You'll get a fit of the giggles.

HELEN   I promise.

Pause.

CHARLES Like two statues?
  HELEN Like two statues.

> CHARLES *smiles and starts slowly to assume the posture of a discus thrower. His movements are very graceful. When he has finished and is in position, the chime of a clock is heard offstage.*
>
> HELEN *now begins to assume the figure of Diana disturbed at her ablutions. When she has done so — the face angled away, one arm shielding her breasts, the hand of the other masking her crotch — she also 'freezes' her position. A second chime is now heard offstage.*
>
> *The stage lights should try to hold and whiten the two forms briefly.*

Scene 6: Eleven O'Clock

The room is now quite dark. An effect of moonlight across it; from time to time car lights sweep it from left to right like a lighthouse beam. A clothes horse has been placed behind the bedspread at centre stage; white shirts, pale blouses are draped along it. HELEN *is sitting on the bedspread;* CHARLES *stands at front of stage, looking towards the audience.*

HELEN I don't know whether to laugh or cry.

> *Pause.*

CHARLES Obvious things were always my . . . Achilles heel. But that's the trouble with intellectuals. They never . . . think.

HELEN Perhaps that's why I love you.

CHARLES (*Thinks*) I could nip next door, and borrow a match from the old couple. He looked like a pipe-smoker. (*Pause*) I'm sure they light fires.

HELEN I'm sure they're sound asleep. You'd only frighten them. (*Pauses; fondly*) You are a Dimwit.

CHARLES I could put my shoes on again, and look for a shop.

HELEN (*Considers this*) I can't risk it. You'd never find your way home.

CHARLES Home? (*He looks at her*)

HELEN Home.

> *Pause*

CHARLES (*Quotes*) 'In such a night as this . . . ' (*Pause; can't remember*) 'In such a night . . . '

HELEN Close your eyes, little hedgehog.

CHARLES Why?

HELEN You'll see. (*Pause*) Close.

60

CHARLES closes his eyes, covers his face with his hands.
*HELEN gets up, goes to tea-chest, finds a match and
lights a waxed taper. She moves around the room,
touching the candles she places here and there in
groups and rows with the taper. When she has finished,
and the room is decorated with them, she blows out the
taper. Pause. She returns to the bedspread and kneels
on it.*

You can look now.

*CHARLES opens his eyes, looks at her. He's mystified;
he may have been expecting her to have removed part
of her clothing.*

Well?
CHARLES Very well. (*Pause*) Never weller.
HELEN I knew I had a match somewhere. Candlelight is so
. . . softly spoken.
CHARLES Yes. (*Pause*) Yes, it is.
HELEN I love to watch them ripple in the draught. (*Pause*)
There'll be wax-drops on the floorboards to remind us
of our first day. Our first night.

Pause.

CHARLES In such a night as this
When the sweet wind did gently kiss the trees
And they did make no noise, in such a night
Troilus methinks mounted the Trojan walls
And sighed his soul toward the Grecian tents
Where Cressid lay that night. (*Pause*)
In such a night
Stood Dido with a willow in her hand
Upon the wild sea banks, and waft her love
To come again to Carthage.
In such a night . . .
(*Pause*) I used to know it. Off by heart. Word perfect.
(*Pause*) The mind plays tricks.
HELEN Never mind. Poor Dimwit.

CHARLES (*Hesitates a moment, then reaches into a tea-chest*)
Where are they?
HELEN (*Stops him*) No.

Pause.

CHARLES Hedgehog?
HELEN No.
CHARLES (*Looks around bedspread*) Like a Persian carpet.
HELEN (*Looks too, then at clothes horse*) More like a life-raft.
CHARLES Keep us afloat.
HELEN Head above water.
CHARLES Drifting toward . . .
HELEN Land.
CHARLES Fog banks.
HELEN Land.

Pause.

CHARLES Eighty years?
HELEN Minimum.
CHARLES Closer than close?
HELEN As close as skin and bone.
CHARLES As close as cuts and bruises.
HELEN The two of us hand in hand.
CHARLES Eyeball to eyeball.
HELEN Back to back.
CHARLES (*Pause*) This is quite ridiculous.

HELEN *in answer removes his spectacles.*

Now you must be my eyes.
HELEN I'll be your guide-dog. Your labrador.
CHARLES (*Listening*) Your tummy's rumbling.

They both listen.

HELEN The first time we ate together, you kept your hand in
front of your mouth as you chewed your chicken.
CHARLES I was shy. (*Listens*) Rumbles. Borborigni.

HELEN Don't you dare tell me what that word is from.

> *They kneel facing each other.* CHARLES *leans forward, kisses Helen's head here and there: the forehead, top of the skull, above the ears.* HELEN *opens his tie, loosens his collar.*

CHARLES It all has to be kissed. Where the trouble starts. (*To himself*) The place of the skull.

> HELEN *shrugs off her blouse; in bra beneath. Slides shirt off Charles' back. She bends, flicks his nipple with her tongue.*

HELEN Are you going to bring me flowers?
CHARLES Yes
HELEN Fresh ones?
CHARLES Wet ones. (*Pause*) The stalks will wet your skirt. Drops on your lap and linen. Drops in the pale places the sun never sees.
HELEN Close the curtains.
CHARLES We can't be seen.
HELEN (*Staring out towards the audience*) But still.
CHARLES Don't you like moon? (*He touches a sliver of silver stage-light*)
HELEN (*Still looking out*) The darkness seems to be staring in at us.
CHARLES It'll be darker if we close the curtains.
HELEN Not with the candles. (*Pause; she looks round at them*) They're so stubborn; they won't budge. They're dug in. (*Pause*) Look. Even the broken one is lighting.
CHARLES Even the broken one.

> *The chime of a clock heard offstage. Freeze-frame; lights down slowly.*